THE LITTLE BOOK OF ADVICE FOR FRUIT & VEG GARDENERS

First published in Great Britain in 2026 by Hamlyn, an imprint of Octopus Publishing Group Ltd
Carmelite House
50 Victoria Embankment
London EC4Y 0DZ
www.octopusbooks.co.uk

An Hachette UK Company
www.hachette.co.uk

The authorized representative in the EEA is Hachette Ireland, 8 Castlecourt Centre, Dublin 15, D15 XTP3, Ireland
(email: info@hbgi.ie)

This material was previously published in *Ask: The 1000 Most-Asked Questions about Gardening*

Distributed in the US by
Hachette Book Group
1290 Avenue of the Americas,
4th and 5th Floors
New York, NY 10104

Distributed in Canada by
Canadian Manda Group
664 Annette St., Toronto,
Ontario, Canada M6S 2C8

ISBN: 978-0-60064-022-6
eISBN: 978-0-60064-023-3

A CIP catalogue record for this book is available from the British Library.

Printed and bound in China.

10 9 8 7 6 5 4 3 2 1

Publisher: Lucy Pessell
Designers: Isobel Platt & Alicia House
Editor: Katie Button
Assistant Editor: Samina Rahman
Production Managers:
Lucy Carter & Nic Jones

MIX
Paper | Supporting responsible forestry
FSC® C144853

THE LITTLE BOOK OF ADVICE FOR FRUIT & VEG GARDENERS

DAPHNE LEDWARD

CONTENTS

INTRODUCTION

In the world of gardening, the same questions arise time and time again: how do I sow my own vegetables? What and when should I plant to get the best results? How should I make the most of my garden or outside space?

Drawing on years of experience in gardening, answering thousands of your questions as a panelist and researcher on shows such as BBC's *Gardeners' Question Time*, this book is the distillation of a lifetime of helping gardeners to create productive and fruitful gardens that bring them joy.

Structured by season, and packed full of tips and easy-to-follow advice, find the answers to all of your fruit and vegetable gardening questions, all year round.

Good luck, and good gardening.

SPRING

"Are home-grown vegetables really worth the bother?"

You do not really save money by growing your own vegetables, but you have the advantage of choosing varieties for taste, and it is easy to grow them without pesticides.

"I AM NEW TO VEGETABLE GARDENING. WHAT CROPS SHOULD I START WITH?"

Start with easy crops: lettuce, spring onions (scallions), carrots, turnips, peas and broad (fava) beans, and take it from there.

"HOW DO I KNOW WHEN IT IS WARM ENOUGH TO SOW VEGETABLES?"

Measure the soil temperature. Most vegetable seed will not germinate at a soil temperature lower than 10°C (50°F).

"What is crop rotation?"

This is a method of arranging the garden so that you never grow the same crop in the same ground in two successive seasons. The crop that follows should benefit from the previous one in some way. The purpose is to create healthy growing conditions and avoid a build-up of pests and diseases.

"What is the minimum depth I should dig my vegetable garden?"

A depth of 25–30 cm (10–12 in) is plenty for most crops.

"I AM MAKING A NEW GARDEN ON OLD PASTURE AND THE GROUND IS FULL OF GRUBS. WHAT SHOULD I DO?"

Dig over the areas in which you want to grow vegetables and perennials and leave them rough for a week or two. The birds will do the rest.

“Is a stainless steel spade essential?”

No it isn’t, but if you have one, you must remember to clean and oil it after each use. In general, spend as much as you can afford on your garden tools.

“I find digging physically difficult. How can I rid the soil of weeds before planting without using chemicals?”

Cover the area with black polythene and most weeds will disappear completely in 12 months.

“WHEN IS A ROTAVATOR USEFUL?”

A rotavator will turn over clean soil and break it down into evenly sized pieces, but you should only use one on ground that you have already cleared of perennial weeds, otherwise you will leave pieces of their roots in the ground, which will reshoot.

"WHAT IS MEANT BY TOPSOIL?"

This is the fertile top layer of your soil. It contains humus (rotted organic material) and beneficial organisms.

"WHAT IS SUBSOIL?"

This is the infertile layer of soil underlying the topsoil. You can break it up when you are digging to improve drainage, but take care not to bring it to the top.

"Are worms beneficial to the soil?"

Yes. They work in, and break down, organic material, improving the soil's quality.

"How can I help my sandy soil retain moisture?"

Add plenty of manure or compost every year.

"How can I improve a heavy clay soil?"

Keep adding compost or manure, sharp sand or horticultural grit, and the texture will start to improve.

"WHAT IS MEANT BY NO-DIG CULTIVATION?"

This is when you spread a thick layer of garden compost or farmyard manure on the surface of the ground and leave it for worms and other soil organisms to work in. It gives the soil a light and easy-to-work texture.

"Why should I put lime on the soil?"

Lime 'sweetens' a sour soil, helping to make nutrients available, and increases the alkalinity. Many plants, such as broccoli, asparagus and cabbages, grow best in a limey soil.

"Is it true that I should not put manure and lime on the soil at the same time?"

Lime releases ammonia gas from the manure, making it less effective as a plant food. The usual advice is to add lime in autumn and manure in spring.

"WHAT IS A MULCH?"

A mulch is a soil covering that suppresses weeds and reduces evaporation. Good examples are chipped bark, gravel and black polythene.

"MY SOIL TAKES A LONG TIME TO DRY OUT IN SPRING."

Keep off waterlogged soil or you will damage the structure. Water-retentive soil will require less watering in dry spells.

"I LIVE IN A DRY PART OF THE COUNTRY. WHAT CAN I DO TO CUT DOWN ON WATERING IN SUMMER?"

Use mulches where you can, and add as much organic material to the soil as possible to make it more water retentive. Mulches should always be laid on damp soil.

"There is a thin layer of soil over solid rock in my garden. How can I grow plants successfully?"

Plant in raised beds to give an adequate depth of soil.

“What do the letters N-P-K on fertilizer packets stand for?”

These are the major nutrients - nitrogen (N), phosphates (P) and potash (potassium, K) - which all plants need in the correct quantities for healthy growth.

"My soil flooded badly from a river last summer. What should I do with it now?"

Dig bare ground to break up any pans (hard areas). Most parts will need extra feeding because the fertilizers will have been leached (washed) out.

"WHAT ARE THE WHITE, THREAD-LIKE THINGS I SOMETIMES FIND IN THE GARDEN? THEY SMELL MUSTY."

These are the mycelia of soil-borne fungi and often live within the roots of plants to the benefit of both.

"What does tilth mean?"

This is soil that has been broken down finely to make it suitable for seed-sowing.

"I always end up with a glut of most vegetables. How can I prevent this?"

Avoid the temptation of sowing the whole packet of seeds at once and sow successionally, leaving a few weeks between sowings.

"HOW CAN I ENCOURAGE CROP GROWTHS?"

Encourage the soil to warm up quickly by covering it with black polythene, and cover early crops with fleece or cloches.

"How do I get rid of horsetail in my vegetable garden?"

Horsetail (*Equisetum*) has a deep root system and does not respond well to chemical weedkillers. However, it does not like being chopped off regularly, so if you hoe the tops off as soon as they grow above the ground, the plants will eventually get weaker.

“I grow my own carrots. Why do they always seem to have forked roots?”

Long-rooted carrots need deep soil without large lumps of fresh manure or compost in it. If you have added manure or compost recently, try growing a different crop first, like cabbage. If your soil is stony, you will need to work it thoroughly to remove as many stones as possible before you sow. Stump-rooted and round carrots are best to grow in shallow soils over rock or gravel.

“MY ONIONS ARE ALWAYS SMALL AND DO NOT STORE WELL. WHAT AM I DOING WRONG?”

Feed with a high-nitrogen fertilizer until the bulbs have reached a reasonable size, then change to a high-potash feed.

"WHAT IS MEANT BY CHITTING POTATOES?"

This is when you expose seed potatoes to light in spring to encourage them to produce shoots. This gets the crop off to a good start.

"HOW DEEP SHOULD I SOW VEGETABLE SEED?"

As a rule, smaller seeds, such as those for lettuce and carrots, should be sown at a depth of about 1 cm (½ in), whereas larger seeds need to be about 2.5 cm (1 in) deep. Always check the packet for guidance on both depth and spacing.

"What is a drill?"

This is the shallow channel into which seeds are sown.

"Last year, all my spinach ran to seed. How can I prevent it this time?"

Spinach needs to be grown quickly in moist soil and thinned out so the plants do not crowd each other. Keep the bed well watered and use the thinnings as salad leaves.

"IS THERE AN EASY ALTERNATIVE TO SPINACH?"

Try leaf or spinach beet, which will survive less ideal growing conditions. When cooked like spinach, it tastes quite similar.

"I still have a lot of leeks left over from the winter, but I want the ground for something else. What should I do?"

Dig them up carefully and heel them in (replant them temporarily) in a hole in a vacant part of the garden. They will last for several weeks like this, but will need more cleaning before cooking.

"I want to grow some asparagus. How do I start?"

Dig the bed thoroughly. Add plenty of well-rotted manure and a balanced fertilizer about a week before planting. Buy one-year-old crowns of an all-male hybrid, such as 'F1 Franklin'.

"HOW DEEP SHOULD I PLANT ASPARAGUS CROWNS?"

Plant the crowns in trenches 20 cm (8 in) deep and 30 cm (12 in) wide. To start with, cover the crowns with about 5 cm (2 in) of soil, and gradually fill in the trench as the shoots grow.

"WHEN CAN I START CUTTING ASPARAGUS SPEARS IN MY NEW BED?"

Never cut the first year after planting. In years two and three, you can cut spears sparingly; thereafter, cut as required.

"When should I sow runner beans?"

If you sow them outdoors too soon, the seeds may rot or a late frost could kill the shoots. Either wait until late spring or sow the plants under glass in mid-spring and plant them out when they are about 8 cm (3 in) tall.

"WHY HAVE I NEVER BEEN ABLE TO GROW GOOD RADISHES?"

Radishes need to be sown little and often, grown quickly in good, moist soil, thinned out so the roots can develop, and picked when young and sweet.

"I never have any luck with aubergines (eggplants). What am I doing wrong?"

Aubergines need a long growing season, so you should start the plants off early in a greenhouse or conservatory with some heat. If you're growing outdoors, give them a warm, sunny, sheltered spot.

"MY RHUBARB PLANTS ARE SPINDLY AND PRODUCE FEW STALKS. WHAT CAN I DO?"

Rhubarb needs an open position and deep, rich soil. Feed several times a season with a general fertilizer and keep well watered. Wait until the plants have recovered before pulling the stalks.

"Last year I grew parsnips, but the roots did not form. What am I doing wrong?"

It is essential that you thin parsnip seedlings in stages as soon as they are large enough to handle. If you do not do this, the roots will not have enough space to swell.

"WHICH VEGETABLES COULD I GROW IN AN ORNAMENTAL BORDER?"

Red-leaved lettuce, red cabbage, carrots, rhubarb chard, dwarf runner beans and cauliflowers with yellow or purple curds.

"I like to grow my own herbs but never have much success. Where am I going wrong?"

Most herbs like a free-draining soil and full sun. They also grow well in tubs and window boxes, so if your garden is shady or the soil is heavy, container cultivation may be the answer.

"WHY DO I NEVER HAVE MUCH LUCK GROWING MINT?"

Mint likes cool, moist growing conditions. It is also best grown in pots because it can be invasive grown in open ground. Find a spot in half shade and never let the plants dry out.

“WHAT COMPOST OR SOIL SHOULD I USE TO FILL RAISED BEDS?”

Large raised beds can be filled with good topsoil with some well-rotted manure or garden compost added. Smaller beds are best filled with soil-based compost.

“Can I use multi-purpose compost in my raised beds?”

Yes, but you may have problems. It dries out quickly and generally needs replacing after every crop, so it is best to invest in soil-based compost from the start.

"There are worms in my raised beds. Will they do any harm?"

These may have come in on the roots of plants or in the soil if you have not used a sterilized compost, but they will do no harm at all.

"WHAT ARE THE OPTIMUM DIMENSIONS FOR A RAISED BED?"

Your beds should be no more than 1.2 m (4 ft) wide and 3 m (about 10 ft) long, so that you have good access to the soil from different sides.

"WHAT IS THE BEST DEPTH FOR A RAISED BED?"

Salad leaves and spinach can be grown successfully in a soil depth of no more than about 15 cm (6 in), but most vegetables will do better in beds that are about 30 cm (12 in) deep.

"What varieties should I look for when I'm sowing vegetables in raised beds?"

Look for varieties described as 'patio' or 'baby' vegetables. These mature quickly and produce good-looking vegetables at closer spacings.

"Will kale grow in a raised bed?"

You will need a fairly large raised bed, but the variety 'Pentland Brigg' is worth trying. Sow the seed in late spring and plant them out in another bed in the second half of summer. Space them 38 cm (15 in) apart.

"LAST YEAR I GREW BROAD BEANS IN RAISED BEDS, BUT THEY ALL FLOPPED OVER. HOW CAN THIS BE AVOIDED?"

They will need to be supported. Make a framework of thin canes, woven together so they stay upright, or use brushwood, pushed into the compost.

"WILL (BELL) PEPPERS GROW IN RAISED BEDS?"

They should grow well if you choose types that are specifically named as 'patio' varieties. Space them about 30 cm (12 in) apart.

"Can I grow tomatoes in a raised bed?"

They are difficult to support, but if you plant a hanging basket variety, such as 'Tumbler', around the edge of the bed, you should get a good crop. The middle area can be used for another vegetable.

"Will garlic grow in a raised bed?"

Garlic does grow well in raised beds, but it needs a long growing season. Plant in early spring, or wait and plant in autumn.

"COULD I GROW COURGETTES (ZUCCHINI) IN A RAISED BED?"

Raised beds are ideal for courgettes and marrows, because the plants can be allowed to hang over the sides. Space them at least 45 cm (18 in) apart for best results.

"CAN I GROW RUNNER BEANS IN RAISED BEDS?"

Climbing beans are tricky to grow in smaller raised beds because they are difficult to support adequately. Dwarf runner beans and French beans are excellent for this type of cultivation, though.

"IS IT SENSIBLE TO TRY GROWING POTATOES IN A RAISED BED?"

You will need a fairly large, deep bed because the tubers should be planted about 30 cm (12 in) apart and 12 cm (5 in) deep. Remember, too, that you will have to earth up the potatoes as they grow. Grow an early variety, like 'Swift', so you can use the bed for something else later in the season.

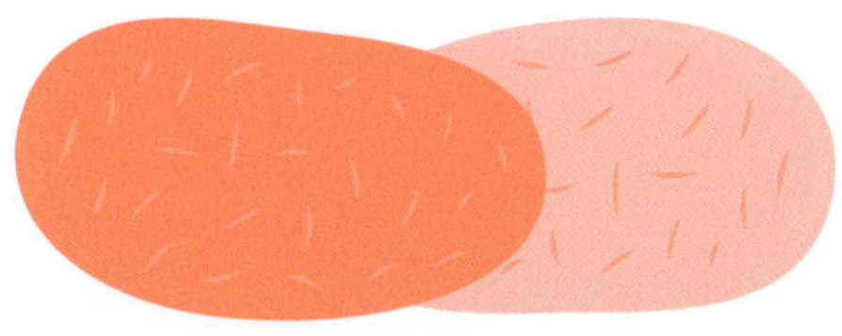

"Which is the best variety of lettuce to grow in a raised bed?"

'Little Gem' is possibly still the best, or you could grow a cut-and-come-again type like 'Salad Bowl'.

"I AM AWAY FROM HOME A LOT. HOW CAN I KEEP MY RAISED BEDS WATERED ADEQUATELY?"

A soaker hose and an electronic timer connected to an outside tap will take all the hard work out of keeping the beds damp.

"WHAT SHOULD I USE TO FEED MY RAISED BEDS?"

Top-dress with a general fertilizer two weeks before sowing or planting in spring, then water with a soluble feed once or twice a week throughout the growing season (in addition to regular watering).

"How often should I change the compost in a raised bed?"

If you are using soil-based compost, you will not need to change it for several seasons, but it will require regular topping up, as you remove some soil every time you remove a plant.

"How can I stop birds digging in my raised beds and throwing the compost everywhere?"

Birds often dig in raised beds looking for insects and similar food. If it becomes a problem, you may need to make a frame and cover the beds with fleece or netting.

"WHAT IS A ROOTSTOCK?"

All fruit trees, like apples, pears and plums, are grafted on to a different root, which modifies the growth. For instance, M27 is a dwarfing apple rootstock; 'Stella' is a semi-dwarfing cherry stock.

"I bought an apple tree supposed to be suitable for a small garden, but it has grown enormous. Who is to blame?"

You may have planted it too deep. The kink in the stem near the base, which is where it was grafted, should be well clear of the soil.

"I have seen fruit trees for sale with the roots wrapped in elastic mesh. How do I plant these?"

The supplier will probably tell you to leave the net on, but if the tree is dormant it will establish better if you cut it off and spread out the roots.

"I LOVE APPLES AND PEARS, BUT HAVE A SMALL PLOT. CAN I HAVE A FRUIT TREE?"

'Family' fruit trees have two or more varieties on one tree, so will give you a mini-orchard. Otherwise, consider cordons, fan-trained and espalier trees.

"CAN YOU RECOMMEND A REALLY NICE PEAR?"

Try 'Concorde'. It is self-fertile and produces huge crops early in its life.

"What is meant by self-fertile?"

Many fruit trees need the pollen from another variety to set a crop. A self-fertile tree will produce a crop without the need for cross-pollination.

"Will an apple tree pollinate a pear?"

No. Apples will only pollinate apples, pears only pears, and so on.

"IS THERE A FRUIT TREE OR BUSH THAT WILL GROW AGAINST A SHADY WALL?"

The cooking cherry 'Morello' can be grown in shade. Blackberries and blackberry hybrids (such as the loganberry or tayberry) will also tolerate all but the densest shade.

"BIRDS ALWAYS EAT ALL MY CHERRIES. HOW CAN I STOP THEM?"

It is impossible to prevent birds from getting the lion's share of fruit on a tall cherry tree. Try netting some lower branches before the fruit starts to ripen.

"When should I prune raspberries?"

Prune summer-fruiting raspberries after fruiting, and autumn-fruiting varieties in spring.

"Which raspberry canes should I prune?"

Completely remove those that have borne fruit, and also any short, weak canes. Tall canes can be cut back slightly in spring for easier access to the crop.

"All my old gooseberry bushes had mildew every year, so I have taken them out. Are any varieties more mildew resistant?"

The varieties 'Invicta' and 'Jubilee' are both resistant and produce huge crops.

"Is it necessary to cover strawberry beds with straw? I cannot get hold of any."

Straw is traditionally used to keep the fruit off the ground and protect it from dirt. You can plant through black polythene or landscape fabric just as effectively.

“I’VE LET MY BLACKCURRANT BUSHES GET OUT OF HAND. WHAT SHOULD I DO?”

Sacrifice the fruit on one or two bushes for a season by cutting them back to ground level. New shoots will appear over summer, and these will fruit next season.

“HOW DO I PRUNE A BLACKCURRANT BUSH TO KEEP IT HEALTHY?”

Remove about one-third of the old shoots every year. This will encourage new growth from low down and keep the bush young.

“I have grown some melon plants in the greenhouse. Can I plant them outdoors in summer?”

Most melon varieties will fruit satisfactorily only at higher temperatures, approximately 21°C (70°F), and need greenhouse cultivation. If you have a warm, sheltered spot in full sun, you could try one or two plants.

"I've grown a peach from a stone. Will I ever get any fruit?"

Productive peach trees grow well from stones. Train it on a sunny wall as a fan and it will, eventually, bear fruit.

"Can I grow an apple from a pip?"

Yes, but it will not come true to the apple variety the pip came from - and unless you bud it on to a dwarfing rootstock, it will make a big tree and take many years to fruit.

"ARE 'PATIO' FRUIT TREES WORTH GROWING?"

These are generally grafted on to dwarfing rootstocks and can be quite weak. You will get better results if you plant a tree on a normal rootstock in a large half-barrel filled with soil-based compost.

"HOW CAN I GROW A QUINCE?"

The quince makes an attractive, ornamental tree. Choose the variety 'Vranja' for a good crop of delicious fruit.

"My fig tree produces a lot of small fruits in late summer. Why do they never come to anything the following spring?"

Remove all embryo fruit after harvesting the figs, but retain any that are about the size of a pea, because these will start to develop the following spring.

"I have inherited some apple trees that have been hard pruned every year and do not produce much fruit. Can I rejuvenate them?"

Mature fruit trees need little pruning, other than the removal of weak, dead and crossing branches. Follow this rule and do not prune the tips. The trees will start to fruit again.

"MY FLOWERING CHERRY HAS GROWN OVER A FLOWER BORDER. WHEN SHOULD I CUT IT BACK?"

Members of the cherry family, such as ornamental and fruiting cherries, plums, peaches, nectarines and the like, should be pruned during warmer times of year (late spring to early autumn) to avoid infection with fungal diseases.

“What is nibbling the edges of the leaves of my peas and broad (fava) beans?”

This damage is caused by the pea and bean weevil. Usually the problem is not serious enough to make spraying with an insecticide necessary.

“The tops of my broad (fava) beans get full of blackfly every year.”

Remove the shoots once the first beans start to set. Broad bean tops can be cooked as a delicious green vegetable.

“I DO NOT LIKE USING CHEMICALS, BUT MY VEGETABLE GARDEN HAS JUST ABOUT EVERY PEST AND DISEASE THERE IS. WHAT CAN I DO?”

Keep all your crops covered with fleece or other plant protection sheeting from sowing to harvesting as a barrier to all manner of nasties.

"Every year my carrots are rendered inedible by little white maggots in the roots. What should I do?"

Choose a carrot-fly resistant variety, like F1 'Flyaway'. Carrots in raised beds are less likely to be affected because the adult flies home in at ground level.

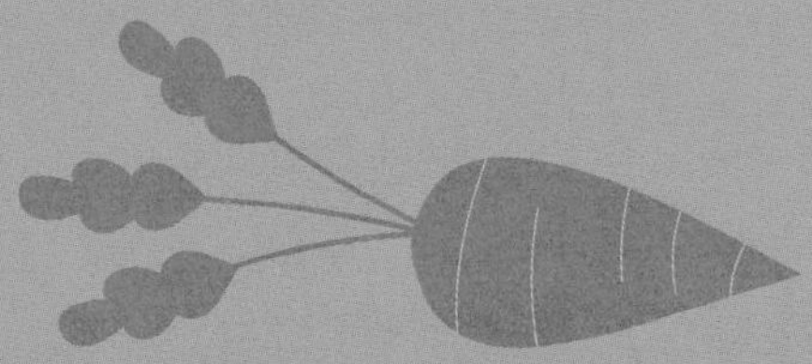

"I sowed a row of early peas a few weeks ago, but nothing has appeared. Are they dead?"

Mice and birds will eat the seed almost as soon as you sow it. Cover immediately with fleece or another transparent crop-protection material.

"LAST YEAR ALL MY ONIONS HAD WHITE ROT. IS THERE ANYTHING I CAN TREAT THE SOIL WITH BEFORE PLANTING MY SETS THIS SPRING?"

Unfortunately not. You will need to grow your onions (and any ornamental alliums) in a completely different part of the garden for at least eight years.

"HOW CAN I KEEP RABBITS OUT OF MY VEGETABLE PATCH?"

Surround your patch with wire netting, buried to a depth of at least 30 cm (12 in). To cut down on cost, divide the area into smaller beds and protect those containing crops that rabbits like most, such as lettuce, carrots, peas and spinach.

SUMMER

"Can I eat the fruit on my *Passiflora caerulea?*"

They are edible but not particularly tasty – although they do make good wine.

"I planted a new asparagus bed last year, and there are a good lot of spears coming through. Can I start cutting them now?"

You can take one or two, but the majority should be left for another year, or you will weaken the plants.

"DO I NEED A PROPER ASPARAGUS KNIFE TO CUT THE SPEARS?"

No, any sharp, long-bladed knife will do.

"WHAT HEIGHT SHOULD ASPARAGUS SPEARS BE BEFORE I CUT THEM?"

They need to be 10–12 cm (4–5 in) long.

"MY ASPARAGUS SPEARS APPEAR A FEW AT A TIME. HOW CAN I GET ENOUGH FOR SOME DECENT SERVINGS?"

Cut each spear when it is ready and store in the salad drawer of your refrigerator until there are enough. They will last several days here.

"When should I stop cutting asparagus?"

Stop cutting no later than midsummer, so the plants have time to recover.

"Should I pinch out my runner beans when they reach the tops of their supports?"

Yes. If you do not, they will hang down over the shoots twined round the supports. However, they will still produce beans, so it will not affect the yield in the long run.

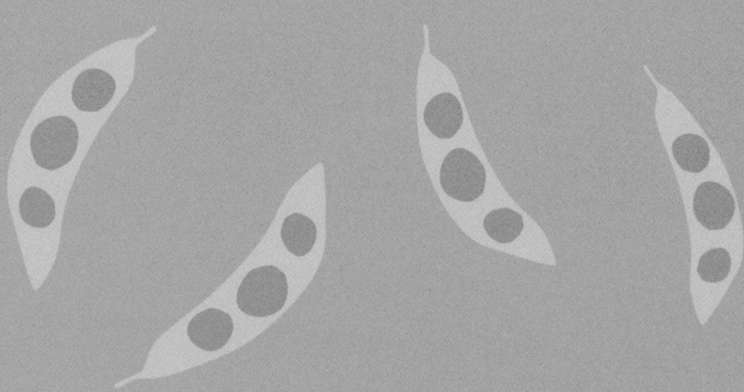

"Can I grow runner beans in a container?"

Yes. Use a deep container, such as a half-barrel, so that you can push the supporting canes in far enough. These should be tied together at the top to form a wigwam.

“Many of my broad (fava) beans have a black mark where they were fastened to the pod. What is this?”

This is a sign that they are too old to be palatable, and the skins will be tough. Pick when the beans are young, bright green and sweet.

“Is it true you can eat young broad beans in their pods?”

Yes. They are delicious, almost like asparagus.

“MY MAINCROP PEAS HAVE FINISHED AND I WANT TO SOW SOME MORE AS A FOLLOW-ON. CAN I USE THE SAME VARIETY?”

No. They will mature too late to set a crop. Sow an early variety, such as 'Feltham First'.

"WHY DO MY BEETROOT (BEET) SOWINGS ALWAYS COME UP TOO THICK?"

This is because each seed of many varieties is actually a cluster of seeds. Sow two seeds 10 cm (4 in) apart to make thinning easier, or grow a more modern variety, like 'Monopoly', which produces seeds singly.

"Why do I never get tight Brussels sprouts?"

'Blown' sprouts are usually caused by the plants whipping around in strong wind. Grow them in a sheltered place, plant deeply, and firm the plants as they grow. Support them with canes if they are grown in exposed situations.

"HOW CAN I PREVENT SCABBY POTATOES?"

Common scab does not affect the taste and cooking qualities of the crop. Grow a resistant variety, such as 'Wilja', and do not lime the soil.

"How can I stop spinach running to seed?"

Sow thinly, thin out the seedlings, keep moist and pick while young. Use the thinnings in salads.

"My onions always have thick necks and don't store well. What can I do?"

Use a high-potash fertilizer instead of a nitrogen-rich one. Sow the seed less deeply in future.

"CAN I GROW WATERCRESS IN MY POND?"

Yes, but it can become contaminated if your pond is not scrupulously clean. Grow land cress instead, which is similar, but is grown in the vegetable garden.

"Why are my onions running to seed?"

This often happens if something happens to check their growth, such as a long dry spell early in the season or a cold spell in late spring. Use these onions first because they will not keep.

"My Jerusalem artichokes are getting tall and take the light from the crops near them. Can I shorten the stems?"

They can be shortened back a little, but if you cut them back too hard, the size of the tubers will be affected. Move them to a more suitable position next year.

"Can I grow a fig tree outdoors in a pot in my small garden?"

Grow *Ficus carica* 'Brown Turkey' in a big tub (a half-barrel is ideal) filled with soil-based compost. Stand the tub on bricks so the plant does not root through the drainage holes into the soil underneath.

"WOULD HERBS THRIVE IN A HANGING BASKET?"

Yes. Herbs make ideal basket plants. Pinch or cut back regularly to keep them neat.

"WHAT IS A SENSIBLE NUMBER OF VEGETABLES TO GROW IN MY 1.8 x 2.4 M (6 x 8 FT) GLASSHOUSE?"

Three cordon tomatoes, such as 'Shirley', two sweet peppers, one cucumber and a hot pepper should fit in and give you enough of each over summer without creating a glut.

"Can you recommend a good aubergine (eggplant) for my greenhouse?"

F1 'Moneymaker' is early, reliable and a heavy cropper. These are regularly sold as plants in the garden outlets in late spring and early summer for potting on at home.

"Can I grow courgettes (zucchini) in the greenhouse?"

Yes, but they take up a lot of room and they grow quite happily outdoors.

"What is the best way to support cordon tomatoes in growing bags in the greenhouse?"

Tie one end of a piece of twine round the bag, close to each plant, and the other end to the roof framework of the greenhouse. Twist each plant loosely round the string as it grows.

"MY TOMATO PLANTS PRODUCE LONG FLOWER TRUSSES, BUT WHY DO SO FEW OF THE FLOWERS SET AND PRODUCE FRUITS?"

This is usually because of poor pollination. Tap the supports or mist the plants at midday.

"WHEN SHOULD I START FEEDING MY TOMATOES?"

Start regular feeding as soon as the first truss is setting.

"What is the best feed for a grapevine?"

Tomato feed will help to produce good crops of large grapes.

"Why are my greenhouse melons slow to ripen?"

Reduce the watering once they reach a good size.

"I have a peach in a pot in the greenhouse. It flowers profusely, but why do most of the fruits drop off before ripening?"

You may be forgetting to water regularly. Otherwise, it possibly needs repotting into a bigger container.

"CAN YOU SUGGEST A SIMPLE PROJECT TO GET MY THREE-YEAR-OLD DAUGHTER INTERESTED IN GROWING THINGS?"

Cut the top off a carrot, place it in a little water in a saucer and watch the ferny leaves sprout.

"What plants might my children be able to grow from pips and stones?"

Try apples, pears, peaches, avocados, grapes, dates and lychees. All these can be germinated in multi-purpose compost.

"My children want to grow something really useful indoors. What do you suggest?"

Buy them some packets of edible sprouting seeds. Start with a glass jar and some muslin to grow them in. If they remain interested in a month or two, buy them a proper seed sprouter.

"MY CHILDREN WANT TO SEE WHAT HAPPENS WHEN THEY PLANT A PEANUT."

This is a fascinating plant, producing a shoot rather like a pea. After flowering, it bends over and buries itself into the compost, and then the peanut pod forms below the surface.

"Can you suggest something I can amuse my three grandchildren with when they stay with me for their summer holidays?"

Give them a tomato plant each and have a competition to see who grows the most fruit by weight. Make the prize something horticultural, and the winner could be hooked on gardening for life.

"What is damaging the stalks of my raspberries just below the flowerhead?"

Blossom weevils will partially sever stalks of strawberries and raspberries in this way before laying their eggs in the buds. Pick off and destroy the buds.

"What are the nasty, worm-like creatures in my potatoes?"

They are wireworms, which can ruin a potato crop. Dig the soil where the potatoes are to be planted several times during winter to expose these pests to birds.

"ONE OF MY APPLE TREES HAS PATCHES OF DEFORMED BARK, WHICH PEEL OFF TO REVEAL BARE WOOD. WHAT IS WRONG?"

Apple canker is a serious disease. Cut off the affected branches to clean wood.

"WHY ARE MY PEAS COVERED IN WHITE, POWDERY PATCHES?"

This is powdery mildew. Spray with a fungicide suitable for edible crops as soon as you see it. Badly affected plants should be taken up and disposed of (not composted).

"WHAT CAN I DO TO PREVENT MY PEAS BECOMING MAGGOTY?"

These are the larvae of the pea moth. Avoid growing mid-season crops, which are usually the worse affected.

"My outdoor tomatoes always start to rot towards the end of summer. What causes this?"

Potato blight also affects tomatoes. You will avoid this if you grow them in a greenhouse or conservatory.

"Many of my apples have brown, ribbon-like scars on the peel. What is wrong with them?"

Control apple sawfly by destroying all affected fruit. The grubs drop from the fruit to the ground in summer, so keep the soil clean and hoe frequently to expose the pupae to birds.

"MY PEAR TREE STARTED TO DIE OVERNIGHT AND LOOKS AS IF IT HAS BEEN BURNED. WHAT IS WRONG?"

This sounds like fireblight, a devastating disease that can affect any member of the rose family. Cut off and burn affected branches immediately. Remove badly affected specimens completely.

"My parsley has turned a reddish-brown and stopped growing. What is the cause of this?"

Root aphids affect many crops, including lettuce and members of the carrot family, like parsley. Do not grow similar crops in the same soil as affected plants.

"Every year, my cabbages, Brussels sprouts and broccoli are destroyed by caterpillars. How can I prevent this?"

The caterpillars of the cabbage white butterfly can ruin a crop. Cover the crops with fleece as soon as you spot the first adult butterfly, and keep them covered for the rest of the season.

"WHAT IS CAUSING THE LITTLE HOLES IN THE LEAVES OF MY TURNIPS?"

Flea beetles. Spray with an insecticide or cover with fleece for the life of the crop.

"MANY OF MY CABBAGES HAVE DIED. WHEN I PULLED THEM UP, THE ROOTS WERE EATEN AND FULL OF MAGGOTS. WHAT ARE THEY?"

These are the larvae of the cabbage root fly. Surround the young plants with discs made of roofing felt or heavy-duty polythene so that the adult flies cannot lay their eggs near the plants.

"WHY ARE ALL MY GREENHOUSE TOMATOES DEVELOPING BLACK SPOTS ON THE BOTTOM OF THE FRUITS?"

This is blossom end rot, caused by a lack of calcium in the compost. Erratic watering makes the problem worse. Always water thoroughly and regularly, and make sure your tomato feed contains calcium.

"Why are my leeks covered with orange spots?"

This is leek rust. Pull up and destroy all affected plants, and grow your onions and leeks somewhere else next year.

"Why do my tomatoes never turn red at the top?"

This is a condition known as greenback, caused by too much direct sunlight. It usually occurs in older varieties, like 'Alicante' and 'Moneymaker'. Grow an F1 hybrid and shade the greenhouse.

"HOW CAN I STOP MY GREENHOUSE VINE GETTING COVERED WITH MILDEW EVERY YEAR?"

Increase the ventilation as much as possible and spray with a fungicide suitable for edible crops every fortnight from late spring.

AUTUMN

“When is the best time to dig vacant land?”

Dig it in autumn so that the winter weather can break it down.

"What is green manure?"

This is a temporary crop of a quick-growing plant, such as rye grass or mustard, which is dug in while still green. It improves soil texture and adds some nutrients.

"ARE THERE ANY GREEN MANURE CROPS I CAN SOW IN AUTUMN?"

Field beans can be sown in autumn. When they are dug in next year, they will fix nitrogen in the soil, meaning you need to add less high-nitrogen fertilizer. You can also sow Hungarian rye and tares. Look on the internet for suppliers.

"I USE THE NO-DIG METHOD OF CULTIVATION IN MY VEGETABLE PLOT. CAN I STILL USE GREEN MANURES?"

Yes. Cut down the tops at the appropriate time and plant through them. The worms will incorporate the manure into the soil.

"I sowed some mustard as a green manure in the summer. What do I do now?"

Mustard should be allowed to grow for one to two months before digging in. Wait about a month before replanting, or allow the soil to rest over winter and plant in spring.

"A friend of mine uses sawdust as a soil improver. Is this a good thing?"

Some sawdust can be added to the soil as an improver, but too much will upset the soil's texture and rob it of nitrates as it rots.

"How can I test the pH (acidity or alkalinity) of my soil?"

A soil-testing kit will give you reasonably accurate readings, but for really precise results, you need to send samples to a soil-testing laboratory.

"THE SOIL IN PARTS OF MY VEGETABLE GARDEN HAS BECOME COMPACTED. WHAT IS THE BEST WAY OF DEALING WITH THIS?"

Divide the area in half. Take out a trench of soil, one spade deep, at the beginning. Fork over the base. Dig the next trench, putting the soil in the first one. Continue to the end of the area, then turn around and work back to the beginning, filling in the final trench with the soil from the first.

"How can I avoid compacting my soil when I'm digging in autumn?"

Don't work when the soil is wet, and try not to walk in the same place every time. If you need to plant while the soil is wet, stand on a plank to spread your weight.

"MY GRANDFATHER DIDN'T USE CONCENTRATED FERTILIZERS ON HIS SOIL, AND HE HAD WONDERFUL FLOWERS AND VEGETABLES. WHY DO I NEED THEM?"

It is possible to keep the soil in good condition by using animal manure or garden compost, but you need a lot of it: about 50 litres per 5 sq m (11 gallons per 50 sq ft) of farmyard manure, or twice as much garden compost. Although this is traditionally applied before digging in autumn, it is better added in the spring so the nutrients are not wasted.

"I WANT TO KILL WEEDS WITH GLYPHOSATE BEFORE DIGGING A NEW PIECE OF GROUND THIS AUTUMN. IS IT SAFE TO DO THIS?"

Yes. Glyphosate is neutralized when it is in contact with soil. Just make sure all the weeds are completely dead before starting to dig.

"I want to get mechanized with my vegetable gardening. Is rotavating as good as digging?"

Not really. It is unlikely to work the soil as deep as digging, and it can cause compaction if used when the soil is wet. Furthermore, it will not leave the ground rough enough for frost to penetrate properly to improve the structure over winter.

"Does lime do anything other than alter the pH of the soil?"

The calcium it contains is a plant food. It also releases other plant foods from organic matter and can discourage pests and diseases.

"WHICH PESTS AND DISEASES CAN BE MANAGED BY ADDING LIME TO THE SOIL?"

Slugs, wireworms and leatherjackets do not like lime. Clubroot disease can be curbed by periodic liming.

"Should I lime flower borders as well as the vegetable plot?"

It depends on what you want to grow and how acid the soil is. Most ornamental plants prefer neutral soil, but wallflowers (*Erysimum*), pinks and carnations (*Dianthus*), delphiniums and clematis do best in alkaline conditions.

"WHEN I HAVE APPLIED LIME ONCE, WHY DO I HAVE TO DO IT AGAIN FROM TIME TO TIME?"

Rain gradually washes lime out of the soil, so it becomes more sour. In addition, adding large quantities of bulky manure regularly will increase the rate at which soil becomes acid.

"When should I apply fish meal to my vegetable garden?"

You can add it in autumn, before planting out overwintering crops, or in spring.

"What are cocoa shells used for?"

They can be used as a mulch or dug in as a soil improver before planting. As a mulch, the shells can become soggy during wet periods, so are best used around woody plants, like trees, shrubs, roses and fruit.

"I bought a variegated lemon tree this summer. The label said it was hardy, so can I leave it outside in winter?"

Citrus trees are usually hardy to only a couple of degrees of frost. If you live in an area that is likely to get spells colder than this, it would be wise to give it winter protection.

"When should I plant a container-grown, fan-trained peach tree?"

From early to mid-autumn is the best time, but you can plant later in the year if conditions are mild.

"HOW MUCH SPACE SHOULD I ALLOW BETWEEN A FAN-TRAINED PEACH AND A FAN-TRAINED NECTARINE?"

Leave about 4 m (12 ft) between trees to allow for growth.

"CAN I PROPAGATE FROM MY RASPBERRY PLANTS?"

If the plants are young and healthy, you can replant suckers in late autumn.

"WHAT'S THE BEST WAY TO MAKE SOME NEW BLACKBERRY PLANTS?"

By layering. Bury the tip of a healthy shoot of this season's growth in early autumn and peg it down to keep it firm. The tip will root and may be severed from the parent plant and planted in early autumn next year.

"Is autumn a good time to plant strawberries?"

The best time to plant bare-root strawberry plants is between late summer and mid-autumn. Container-grown plants can be put in at any time when the weather is suitable.

“What shall I do about the masses of runners on my strawberry plants?”

These can be removed in autumn, if you have not already done so, to keep the parent plants individual. However, if the runners are left to root into the bed, you will get a much heavier crop next season, although many of the fruits will be smaller.

"When should I cut back fruited strawberry plants?"

Late summer or early autumn is the time to cut back the plants and generally tidy up the bed.

“HOW CAN I TAKE BLACKCURRANT CUTTINGS?”

Take cuttings, 25 cm (10 in) long, from healthy, heavy-bearing bushes in autumn. Bury them so only two buds show above the soil.

"I have some good gooseberry bushes I raised from cuttings last year. What pruning do they need now?"

Remove the lower branches so that the bush grows on a short 'leg', and cut back the side-shoots you retain by about half. Remove the leading shoot completely.

"I HAVE BEEN GIVEN A SMALL PLANT OF A WORCESTERBERRY (*DIVARICATUM* HYBRID), WHICH LOOKS LIKE A CROSS BETWEEN A GOOSEBERRY AND A BLACKCURRANT. HOW DO I LOOK AFTER IT?"

This is actually a species of currant, but is thorny and is treated like a gooseberry.

"WHEN CAN I EXPECT MY MELONS TO RIPEN?"

They usually ripen from early autumn onwards, depending on variety.

“How do I grow a kiwi fruit?”

These plants, *Actinidia deliciosa*, are deciduous climbers, and they need quite a lot of space. You will either need both a female and a male plant for fertilization, or you can choose a self-fertile cultivar, like ‘Jenny’. Plant against a sheltered, sunny wall or fence.

“WHAT ARE MIRABELLE PLUMS USED FOR?”

These sweet mini plums can be used in the same way as ordinary plums or made into wine.

“I have limited room to grow fruit trees and would like to plant some cordons. What is the minimum space between plants?”

Allow 75 cm (30 in) between trees.

"Why do my apple trees produce a lot of top growth every year?"

You are probably winter-pruning too hard. Leave them unpruned this year and see if growth slows down.

"I LOVE APPLES BUT ONLY HAVE ROOM FOR ONE TREE. ARE THERE ANY SELF-FERTILE VARIETIES?"

If you have good soil, try 'Self-Fertile Cox'. Alternatively, plant 'Redsleeves', which is partly self-fertile.

"Which is the best culinary crab apple?"

Malus 'John Downie' has attractive flowers and crops heavily. The fruit makes good jelly.

“ARE THE FRUITS ON MY ‘MAYPOLE’ BALLERINA APPLE TREE EDIBLE?”

Yes. They will make a pinkish-red jelly.

“My local nursery offers step-over apples. What are these?”

These are effectively single-tier espaliers trained horizontally about 30 cm (12 in) above the ground. They are pruned like espaliers in late summer or early autumn, and make an attractive edging to a bed or border.

"When I prune apple and pear trees, how can I identify a fruit spur?"

Fruit spurs are short, twiggy branches bearing fat buds that will bear fruit. They produce no extension growth, so will get no longer.

"WHEN ARE THE FRUITS OF A MEDLAR RIPE?"

Pick the fruits in late autumn and leave them for many weeks until they turn brown. This process is known as bletting.

"Can I grow new potatoes for midwinter?"

If you have an unheated greenhouse, cold frame or conservatory, you can have new potatoes on Christmas Day (in the northern hemisphere). In late summer or early autumn, buy seed potatoes that have been specially treated (most big seed companies offer these). Put two or three on a layer of multi-purpose compost in a large pot and fill the rest of the pot with compost. Keep damp but do not overwater, and shoots will soon appear.

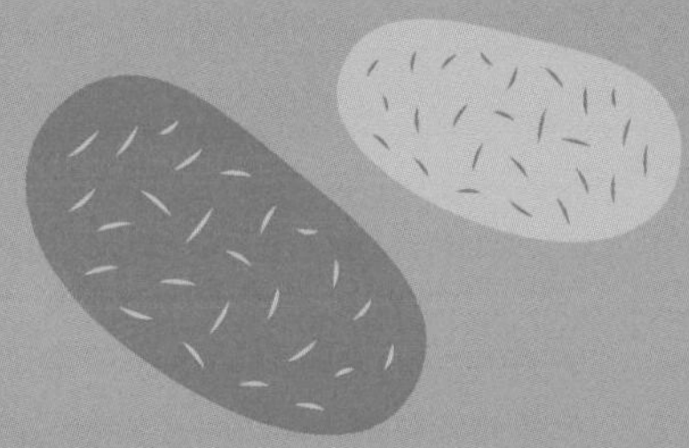

“WHEN SHOULD I LIFT MAINCROP POTATOES FOR STORAGE?”

The best time is early to mid-autumn, but if the weather is wet, you may have to lift later.

“When should I sow overwintering broad (fava) beans and early peas?”

Mid- to late autumn is the best time. Cover them with fleece to protect them from birds.

"When I pulled up my runner beans, the roots looked rather like dahlia tubers. Is this a disease?"

No. Runner beans are, in fact, perennial plants, and if the tuberous roots are protected from frost, they will come up again the following year, although the yield will not be as good.

"AN EXPERIENCED GARDENER TOLD ME I SHOULD NOT REMOVE PEA AND BEAN ROOTS AT THE END OF THE SEASON. WHY?"

These should be left in the ground as a useful source of nitrogen.

"I sowed some perpetual spinach and still have a lot of leaves left. It seems a shame to pull them up. What should I do with them?"

Perpetual spinach is winter hardy. If you cover the crop with fleece, you should be able to pick sparingly throughout winter, and you will get some early pickings next spring, although the plants will eventually run to seed.

"Do I have to lift beetroot (beet) in autumn?"

If you protect the crop with fleece or cloches it may survive the winter, but it is likely to be damaged by slugs. If you do not have the space to store the crop, however, it is worth the risk.

"Will my main-crop carrots be all right if I leave them in the ground until I need them?"

They will survive the winter, but so will overwintering pests, such as aphids and carrot fly grubs, so it is better to lift them.

"CAN I USE CLOVES FROM MY HOME-GROWN GARLIC TO GROW ANOTHER CROP NEXT YEAR?"

Yes, as long as they are absolutely disease free.

"I LOVE TURNIP TOPS. CAN I SOW NOW FOR AN EARLY CROP NEXT SPRING?"

Sow a maincrop variety in early autumn for spring greens from early spring onwards.

"WHEN SHOULD I PLANT RHUBARB?"

Traditionally, early spring was the time for planting, but on well-drained soil and in warmer districts, you can plant from late autumn throughout the winter.

"What should I do with globe artichoke plants at the end of the season?"

Remove any unharvested heads and stems and any dead leaves at the base of the plants. Do not plant offsets until spring, or they may rot.

"What is the latest time I can sow winter radishes?"

Late summer is the best time, but you can still sow in early autumn if you have had to wait for space in the vegetable garden.

"I HAVE GROWN SOME SPROUTING BROCCOLI PLANTS. WHEN SHOULD I PLANT THEM IN THEIR FINAL POSITIONS?"

Plant whenever they are ready, from early to late autumn. Protect them against birds.

"HOW FAR APART SHOULD I SPACE SPRING CABBAGE?"

Space plants about 10 cm (4 in) apart and thin out gradually in spring. Use the first thinnings as spring greens.

"Can I sow lettuce in autumn for an early crop next year?"

Choose a winter-hardy variety, such as 'All the Year Round' or 'Winter Density'. In colder areas, the plants will need protection with cloches.

"I HAVE GROWN FAR TOO MANY WINTER SQUASHES. WILL THESE STORE?"

You can keep them in a cool, dry place for several months.

"My parsnips have got brownish-black areas near the top. What caused this?"

This is parsnip canker. It is worse in early-sown crops and acid soil. Lime the area before growing parsnips again, and choose a canker-resistant variety. Do not compost diseased roots.

"WHY DID ALL MY CAULIFLOWERS DEVELOP BROWN CURDS THIS SEASON?"

This is usually a sign of boron deficiency. Add plenty of garden compost in autumn, and apply borax before planting next year.

"My autumn cabbages are covered in whitefly. What can I do?"

Spray with a vegetable insecticide at three-day intervals until the problem is resolved. Do not compost infested leaves.

"Why is my kohlrabi tough and stringy?"

You are leaving it too long before harvesting. The globes should be no more than the size of a tennis ball, and preferably golf-ball size, to be at their best.

“WHAT IS THE BEST WAY TO STORE KOHLRABI FOR THE WINTER?”

Kohlrabi does not store well and should be eaten fresh. Leave plants in the ground until they are needed.

"How long should I expect my tomato plants to last?"

They will last well into the autumn if you look after them properly. Pick the fruit regularly.

“What can I do with the green tomatoes left at the end of the season?”

Ripen them indoors on a sunny windowsill, or put them in a plastic bag with a ripe banana. Remove old plants, growing bags and spent compost immediately and wash the pots (if used) before storing for the winter.

"Many of my tomatoes are struggling to ripen as the leaves are shading the fruit. What should I do?"

Regularly remove and clear up all leaves that are covering the trusses.

"When is the best time to clean out the greenhouse?"

The gap between clearing out vegetables, such as cucumbers and tomatoes, and bringing in your overwintering patio plants is the time for an autumn clean. Wash off any shading and pay particular attention to moss growing between the glass and the glazing bars. Use a greenhouse disinfectant to clean the glass, staging and floor.

"I GREW A PINEAPPLE PLANT FROM THE TOP OF A FRUIT THIS SUMMER. CAN I OVERWINTER IT IN AN UNHEATED GREENHOUSE?"

No. It will probably be too cold. Put it on a sunny windowsill in the house in autumn.

"CAN I SOW ANY VEGETABLES IN AUTUMN IN AN UNHEATED GREENHOUSE?"

Carrots, lettuce, radishes and land cress can be sown now for an early crop.

"Can I plant a grape vine this autumn as shade for my sunny greenhouse?"

Yes, but ideally the vine should have its roots outdoors, so you may have to make a hole somewhere near the base. It should be trained to shade the sunny side only.

WINTER

"HOW SHOULD I WINTER-PRUNE AN OVERGROWN APPLE TREE?"

Remove all but about five, evenly spaced main branches. Then thin out the branches coming from these so there is good air circulation in the head and no shoots are crossing or rubbing against each other.

"I have a peach tree trained against a wall. I am told to keep rain off it in winter to prevent peach leaf curl. What is the best way to do this?"

Erect a temporary cover of heavy-duty plastic sheeting over the top so the rain runs off it to the sides and front. Remove the cover in spring.

"What is a runner bean trench?"

This is a trench at least 30 cm (12 in) deep, which is dug in autumn. Shredded newspaper, kitchen waste (other than cooked food, meat and dairy products) and other organic material can be added throughout the trench. When full, it is covered with soil. As it rots down, it both warms the soil and improves the texture.

"ARE THERE ANY VEGETABLES I CAN SOW NOW?"

In a frost-free greenhouse, you can sow early cabbage, lettuce, summer cauliflowers and leeks for an early crop.

“What can I use my cold frame for in winter?”

Sow salad leaves in autumn, and use the frame to protect them. ‘Amsterdam Forcing’ carrots will germinate in growing bags under a cold frame in late winter.

“I HAVE A HEATED CONSERVATORY. CAN I SOW TOMATO SEED FOR AN EARLY CROP?”

If you can maintain a minimum night temperature of 10°C (50°F), you can sow the seed in a propagator for cropping from early summer onwards.

"Can I get an early crop of strawberries in the greenhouse?"

Pot up some plants from the garden and put them in a light position on the bench or staging. You will get a considerably earlier crop.

"I HAVE BEEN STORING MY MAIN-CROP POTATOES IN OLD COMPOST BAGS. WHY HAVE THEY ALL GONE ROTTEN?"

Potatoes must be stored in opaque, breathable linen sacks. Some seed companies offer these for sale.

"How can I get a supply of mint throughout the winter?"

Pot up a few roots and put them in a warm, light place, such as the conservatory or on the kitchen windowsill. New shoots will soon appear.

"HOW CAN I PREVENT A CONTAINER-GROWN PEACH ON MY PATIO FROM GETTING LEAF CURL EVERY YEAR?"

Move it into a cold greenhouse or conservatory for the winter to keep the rain off it because the spores that cause it are carried in rainwater.

"I tried growing ornamental kale last winter, but they all ran to seed."

Kale will start to flower when the average winter temperature is above normal, which has happened in recent years. There is nothing you can do about it.